R E N E W I N G   Y O U R
Money Mind

How to Go from
Common Cents to Kingdom Wealth

BARBARA R. GALLOWAY

ISBN 978-1-0980-1961-7 (paperback)
ISBN 978-1-0980-1962-4 (digital)

Christian Faith Publishing, Inc.
832 Park Avenue
Meadville, PA 16335
www.christianfaithpublishing.com

Unless otherwise noted, all Scripture quotations are taken from the King James Version of the Bible.

Scripture quotations marked (NIV) are taken from THE HOLY BIBLE, NEW INTERNATIONAL VERSION®, NIV® Copyright© 1973, 1978, 1984, 2011 by Biblical, Inc.™ All rights reserved.

Scripture quotations marked (AMP) are taken from the Amplified® Bible (AMP), Copyright© 2015 by The Lockman Foundation. www.lockman.org.

Printed in the United States of America

What Others Are Saying

"Barbara Galloway graciously shared her monetary wisdom with Mocha Moms, Inc., and our members were so blown away that they begged her to come back and share some more. As such, she has addressed the local chapter of this national support group program two years in a row, and we look forward to her returning next year! As mommies, worrying about money is a foregone conclusion, but Barbara gave us good information when it comes to paying for our children's higher education in addition to teaching our children about money. We loved and appreciated how patiently she answered our endless questions and the confidence she instilled in us to make better decisions. She rocks! I am so glad to see that she has captured the timeless and proven money lessons based on biblical principles into a book. It will be a welcome addition to my resource library."

Brooke N. Hawkins
Marriage Support Program Director
Mocha Moms, Inc.

"This literary composition "Renewing Your Money Mind" is the answer and direction one needs when you are headed for rock bottom. It not only answers your deepest and most asked questions, but it gives you hope and a desire to do better. If you need or are looking for answers—Renewing Your Money Mind is the answer!!!"

Winston Chaney,
RADIO-ONE-WYCB 1340 AM Washington, DC

"In all of life…present, needed, and wanted in every social institution is the common denominator—money. 'Working for your money' is one thing, herein, Barbara so caringly and plainly presents the **how to** regarding the corollary, 'have your money work for you.' Merely reading this excellent work is one thing, studying it and applying it could lead you to financial peace of mind."

Ira G. Turpin, Jr., Financial Advisor, Sr.
Partner & Founder of Turpin Martin Powell, Inc.

"An amazing work, full of practical wisdom, and proven techniques by an author with deep spiritual insights who doesn't just 'talk the talk' but 'walks the walk.' A person who applies these techniques will be better off financially as well as spiritually."

Joel Whitaker, Business Journalist

To my mother, my supporter: You were the first person who taught me how to spend a little, save a little, and to give God his portion. "He only wants one dime from every dollar. You get to keep the other ninety cents!"

To my father, my hero: You are the wisest person I've ever had the pleasure of knowing. Though your mind has waned, your spirit waxes strong, and your lessons and love still guide and fuel me.

CONTENTS

FOREWORD

Renewing Your Money Mind: How to Go from Common Cents to Kingdom Wealth by Barbara Galloway is the ultimate *spiritual financial coaching* written and inspired by a dynamic author and servant of God. In this, her first body of work, Minister Galloway imparts not only her formal training in money matters but most importantly, she does it on a biblical paradigm; eloquently capturing what God meant in his written Word about money. My wife, Felicia, and I have benefited personally and spiritually from Barbara's teachings. She empathizes with all who are having financial challenges and offers her personal testimony and successful keys to overcome this major stronghold to all (Christian and non-Christian). Additionally, we benefited *tangibly* by applying Scriptures and the biblical principles, which changed our attitudes about what God expects from us as financial stewards. *Renewing Your Money Mind* is a kingdom wealth building tool that I recommend highly to all who are seeking a huge return on investment, spiritual and otherwise.

Rev. Dr. Reginald D. Tarver, Th.D.
Pastor, Revelation of Christ Baptist Church (The ROC)

ACKNOWLEDGMENTS

I began writing this book in December 2018 flying home from Chandler, Arizona, where I spoke at the Spiritual Women Anointed by God (SWAG) empowerment workshop, led by the visionary Dr. Sonnet Ford-Grant. After my session, several participants asked me if I had a book, a website, or how they could get more information. Their hunger for more, combined with Dr. Ford-Grant's empowering messages at the SWAG workshops, awakened my dream to write a book that had been deferred for decades. Thank you, Dr. Sonnet, for stirring up my gifts and for encouraging and empowering so many people to tap into their full potential. You helped me birth this book in a way that only *you* could have done. It would never have become a reality if you hadn't set the example.

I also want to thank Sebora Kargbo for selflessly taking time to edit my manuscript, despite your hectic schedule; Brooke "Hawkeye" Hawkins, for your incredible ability to catch the most miniscule of errors and your invaluable creative suggestions; Marilyn Stewart, who not only reviewed the book, but consumed it. After only one read through, you were able to quote from the book liberally.

I was able to write this book because I have been and continue to be transformed by the renewing of my mind. My spiritual maturity is ultimately the result of the Holy Spirit. However, he graced me with the teaching and leadership of several earthly vessels. I would like to thank: Pastor Debra Garner of Purpose Destination Ministries; Pastor Ron Carpenter of Redemption Church; and Apostle Dr. Darryl A. Baccus of Cornerstone Ministries, International.

Finally, there are people whose support and belief in me are literally the wind beneath my wings: My loving husband, John; my encouraging daughter, Maya; my beloved parents, Herman and Bertha, to whom this book is dedicated; my supportive sister, Cheryl; my protective brother, Lenard; my first mentor and cousin Johnnie; my loyal friend Beverley; and other friends and family who have touched my life in a special way. You know who you are.

INTRODUCTION

---

*Do not conform to the pattern of this
world, but be transformed by the
renewing of your mind. Then you will be
able to test and approve what God's will
is—his good, pleasing and perfect will.*
—Romans 12:2 (NIV)

Getting money isn't the key to wealth, *keeping* it is; but
to keep money, you must let go of it. You must let go of
your love for it; your desire for it; your worship of it; your
seeking it at all costs; and its hold on you. "Letting go
of money in order to keep money" seems contradictory
and illogical; and it is, according to society. However, it's a
truth according to God's principles for managing money.
The *only* way to transform your finances is to renew your
mind about money. You must change your mind-set by
learning God's principles.

God is not silent on the subject, with over two thousand Bible verses about money, greed, possessions, and
wealth. There are more Scriptures in the Bible about
money than there are about prayer and faith combined.[1]

Sadly, some people will read the above and think, "The Bible is too confusing" or "I'm not religious" or a thousand other thoughts. Let me ease your mind. First, this book will discuss biblical money principles in a practical way that's easy to understand. Second, it is best that you are not religious (adhering to a moral code governing the conduct of human affairs) but rather that you are open to a new way of being and thinking.

This new way of thinking is necessary if you are to ever achieve financial freedom and kingdom wealth!

What Is Kingdom Wealth?

Kingdom wealth is when you have no concern or worry for the things that money can buy, whether it's food, water, clothing, shelter or any of the other needs or wants of life. It's when you are so content today because you know that tomorrow will take care of itself. It's peace. It's joy. It's contentment. It's when all your needs are met. It's getting to the place where you want nothing. Not because you have everything, but because you are content with what you do have. My daughter's love language is gifts so it's a big deal to her to buy me nice gifts for birthdays and Christmas. When she asks me what I want, I always have the hardest time thinking of something to tell her. I realize it's because I truly do not desire anything, at least not things that money can buy. Because I delight in the Lord, he gives me the desires of my heart. This is a beautiful place to be! It might be hard for you to imagine not wanting *anything*, but that's only because your money mind isn't renewed yet; but hopefully, after reading this book, you'll be well on your way.

However, kingdom wealth is also tangible. It's being in a position where you are taking care of all your needs and wants (which are virtually nonexistent) and yet, you're still able to give, to share, and to bless others financially. It's when you're able to give from your abundance. It's the payoff and riches that result from seeking the kingdom of God and his righteousness. Kingdom wealth is when God allows you to find favor in the eyes of people again and again. When you get that job that you weren't even seeking; when you find the mate that's not perfect, but perfect for you; when your children are blessed and bringing you joy; when you have good physical and mental health; when you have fun, loyal, and treasured friends; and when you have a loving and supportive family. These too represent kingdom wealth. These things are so much more important, rewarding, and life-sustaining than any common dollars and cents you spend chasing. The Bible says:

> *"But Seek ye first the kingdom of God, and his righteousness and all these things shall be added unto you"* (Matt. 6:33).

Kingdom wealth is the "all these things added unto you," which is unlimited, indescribable, and both present and eternal.

Most books about money and finances are long because there are so many topics to cover (i.e., savings, investing, budgeting, insurance, debt, taxes, estate planning, retirement, and so on). The subject can be overwhelming as each topic easily could be its own book. However, *Renewing Your Money Mind* has an entirely different perspective and goal—to change your perspective. For example, unless you change the way you think about debt, even if you eliminate your debt, you'll find yourself right back in it. Most credit repair programs and books tell you how to fix debt or how to repair your credit, but they don't tell you why you're there in the first place. If you don't pull a weed from its source—the root in the ground—it will grow back. Cutting it down isn't enough. This book will help you pull your weeds from the root by renewing your money mind.

The only requirement for reading this book is that you have a desire for a renewed mind, which means thinking beyond the way the world does. A renewed mind leads to a transformed heart, which leads to contentment. I want to see money lose its hold on you; to see you controlling it and not it controlling you. I want you to learn the secret of contentment and the joy of giving. I want you to be found a faithful steward and to have financial freedom; able to pursue your life purpose, dreams, talents and gifts, and not limited by a lack of resources. I want you to be blessed beyond measure. I want to see your money mind renewed so you can go from common cents to kingdom wealth. If any of this is what you want, let's get started!

Helpful hint: The *only* way you can renew your money mind is to agree with what God says about money. I incorporate relevant Bible verses within and at the end of each chapter. Study and memorize those that best speak to your situation.

CHAPTER 1

Change Your Mind$et

For as he thinketh in his heart, so is he.

—Proverbs 23:7

Many people believe that if they just made more money, or if they could hit the Powerball, then all their financial problems would go away. It sounds good. It even sounds logical, but reality says otherwise. Research shows that lottery winners are more likely to declare bankruptcy within three to five years than the average American.[2] And we all know that professional sports players are some of the highest paid people in America. Yet, 78 percent of National Football League (NFL) players are bankrupt or under financial stress within two years of retiring; and 60 percent of National Basketball Association (NBA) players go bankrupt within five years of leaving their sport.[3] It makes you wonder if the famed rapper Notorious B.I.G. was on to something when he penned the song, "Mo Money Mo Problems."

Yes, more money can lead to more problems, such as increased tax liability (the more you make, the more Uncle Sam will take); increased concern about loss of possessions; expectations from family and friends, which can lead to strained relationships, just to name a few. However, let me suggest to you that it isn't "mo' money" that causes "mo' problems," but rather your mindset toward the money you have, whatever the amount.

Your financial situation today is a direct reflection of your earliest attitude and beliefs about money, typically ingrained from childhood. As strange as it may sound, you might be sabotaging your opportunities to obtain wealth or to be financially secure because you don't think you deserve it. Or maybe you have a mindset that living paycheck to paycheck is fine, because that's all you've ever seen. Perhaps it's what you saw your parents do and you have no expectation that it could be any different. Or maybe you think that paying for things with credit instead of cash is a good practice, because that's what you grew up seeing, or no one ever told you there was a better way; and that using credit can be costly. Do you feel uncomfortable or guilty when you have abundance, does it feel wrong, or do you feel undeserving? When this is the case, your money will blow a hole in your pocket; you'll spend it as fast as you get it. As soon as you get some cha-ching, you're looking to see what you can buy! Can you relate to any of these scenarios? If so, you need to change your mindset.

A prime example of a common mindset can be seen in those who grew up during the Great Depression (1929–1939). It's referred to as the worst economic downturn in modern history. During the worst point of it, nearly 25 percent of the US workforce was unemployed. Others had their wages cut or were reduced to part-time.[4] If you know anyone who lived during this time (a parent or grandparent), you probably saw the effect it had on them. They were or are likely to be very frugal, even pack rats, never throwing away anything. My mother and father were five and six years old when the Great Depression ended, and I can never get them to throw away *anything*, no matter how old it is. They also believe in keeping their pantry stocked with canned goods and an extra deep freezer full of frozen food. The mindset of frugality was set for them and many of that generation by this economic event.

The truth of the matter is: *you can never rise above your level of thinking*. What you think about money and how you manage it needs to be elevated; it needs to grow beyond limiting thought patterns and a worldly view. Society says, "Get all you can, any way you can," and "Money buys happiness." We are told "bigger is better" even if we can't afford the bigger things, and that we must "keep up with the Joneses," whoever they are. The best way for us to overcome these limiting mindsets is to start viewing money and wealth the same way God does; after all, he is the creator and provider of wealth—he owns it all!

> *"Both riches and honor come from You, and You rule over all"* (1 Chron. 29:12, AMP).

A Rude Awakening

One night, when my four-year old daughter (who is now an adult) and I came home, I opened our front door and flipped on the light switch; the house remained

19

dark. I tried another light switch, and it didn't work either. Then it hit me like a ton of bricks. The power company had made good on their threats to shut off my electricity due to nonpayment. Thinking quickly, I told my daughter, "Let's play a game. Let's see if we can get ready for bed in the dark, using only a flashlight." None the wiser, she giggled and happily agreed to the challenge. The next day, I negotiated a payment plan with the company and got my power restored. However, one morning, a few months later, I left out for work, but my car was not in its assigned parking space. I ran back in the house and called the police to frantically report my car stolen! After putting me on a brief hold, the police dispatcher returned and said, "Ma'am, your car was repossessed."

What makes the above true story so incredulous is that I had a good job, good income, a bachelor's degree in accounting and a master's degree in business administration from a top ten business school and no student loans. Surely, I knew how to manage *my* finances. As a recently separated, single mom, I made more than enough money for my daughter and I to live comfortably. The problem was my mindset. I always had a penchant for quality things. I never budgeted, or cut corners, clipped coupons, etc. I didn't value money or respect its limits. I figured if I wanted something, I deserved it and would get it. I never told myself "no." I didn't have outrageous spending habits, but they were bad enough to tip the scales—more was going out than was coming in and without a spending plan or budget, there was no way to see or feel the deficit I was creating each month (other than by the harassing phone calls I received from bill collectors). I viewed credit cards as free money to be spent. I knew all about assets, liabilities, balance sheets, income statements and taxes, but all my textbook knowledge was overridden by my childhood mindset around money—that money grew on trees (not literally, but proverbially).

After living this way for a few years, I realized that my mindset around money was sabotaging any chances I had of achieving real wealth and setting a solid financial example for my daughter. So, I set out on a mission to renew my mind and to learn how to manage my money according to God's principles. These principles changed my life and have been the driving force of all my financial decisions. I started tithing, stopped using debt for consumer purchases, saved for my daughter's college (she graduated from a four-year private university loan free), bought a second home, invested in the stock market, maximized my retirement savings, obtained a perfect credit score, and became an even bigger giver. I became an expert in godly financial principles and for the past twenty years have been teaching individuals, couples, and groups these mind-renewing and heart-transforming principles.

I realized that no matter what worldly knowledge I obtained about money and wealth, unless I managed my money according to God's Word, the one who owns it all, I'd never have true wealth or peace in my finances. Changing the way you think about money is *the single greatest thing you can do* to make a difference in your current situation. The good news is, once you replace your false mindset with truth, you can position yourself to obtain and maintain wealth! Let's look at some of the most common false mindsets and a corresponding biblical truth.

False mindset #1: It's easier to buy now and pay later.

When you use credit rather than cash to make consumer purchases (clothing, food, home items, entertainment, electronics, etc.), it allows you to live beyond your means. These things should *always* be paid for with cash (which includes a debit card or personal check) and *never* with a credit card. Using credit causes you to buy beyond your means and increases the chance of impulsive buying. Bottom line, it is not easier to buy now and pay later, for one reason—finance charges!

Finance charges are fees or interest the credit card company charges for the convenience of delaying payment. They are basically lending you the money, which you pay back incrementally. The longer you take to pay it back, the greater interest fees you pay. Don't fool yourself and say, I'll put it on my charge card and pay it in full before interest charges hit. If you were willing to do that, you would have paid in full at the point of purchase. It's too easy to just pay the minimum due each month, which causes you to end up paying for the item twice or three times over. This book will not go deeply into financial applications, as there are plenty of books that do that, but I think it's important that you understand why using debt to purchase items is so bad. So, let's look at this example:

The Cost of Credit

You decide you want a new sofa. Rather than waiting to save up the money for it, you decide to put it on a credit card that already has a $1,500 balance on it from previous purchases. The sofa is $3,000, so your new balance on the credit card is $4,500. The monthly finance charge can be calculated by knowing four things:

Credit card balance = $4,500
Annual Percentage Rate (APR) = 24 percent
Length of the billing cycle = 12 months
Periodic rate = APR divided by billing cycles = .24/12 = 0.02

Your monthly finance charge is $4,500 × .02 = $90

This $90 is in addition to the cost of the items you purchased with the credit card. So, if you pay $150, only $60 goes toward knocking down your balance. The other $90 is the cost of borrowing that you pay the credit card company. So even though you paid your $150, your new balance is $4,440, just $60 less than what it was, because you had to pay the credit card company $90. Next month, you'll have another finance charge to pay based on a balance of $4,440. As long as you have a balance on your credit card you will have to pay finance charges each month and will end up giving the credit card company much more than the original cost of the sofa. It would have been better to not buy the new sofa, or to wait until you had enough cash saved to buy it outright.

When it comes to consumer-type purchases, I strongly advise that you *never* use credit. Train yourself to practice *delayed gratification* and only purchase things when you have enough designated cash to do so. Delayed gratification is defined as the ability to put off fun or pleasure now to gain more fun, pleasure, or rewards later. Research has shown that delayed gratification is one of the most effective personality traits of successful people.[5]

Don't Fall Prey to the New Car Smell

Car salesmen prey on the "buy now, pay later" mindset. They are happy when you walk in the showroom and tell them the maximum car note you're willing to pay. Often, they will even ask you, "So, what car note are you looking for?" This is a trap! They want you fixated on the monthly car note and not on the total cost of the car. Do *not* negotiate the purchase of a car using monthly payments as the sole criteria. They are very creative finding ways to meet your target monthly payment, but in the long run, it will cost you several thousands of dollars, because of longer loan terms. This means you can be financing the car for five, six or seven years! If it takes you that long to pay off a car, then you can't afford it. Get a cheaper one. Always negotiate the price of the car. Most people need to finance a car, as they don't have the cash laying around, but make sure you are considering the total price and not monthly payments. Many financial experts recommend that you *never* buy a new car because as soon as you drive it off the lot, it loses 30 percent of its value, which is called depreciation. However, I take a somewhat softer and more realistic approach—I mean who doesn't want that new car smell at least once in your life. *But* that new smell can be an alluring trap! Buying a car that's a few years old is *always* a better financial move. However, whether buying new or used, heed the helpful hints listed in Appendix A.

In summary, when purchasing consumer goods, buying now and paying later is the most insidious of all money traps! For larger purchases like a car or home, financing is likely necessary and expected, but you should still use wisdom to minimize the cost of borrowing.

TRUTH #1: "The rich rule over the poor, and the borrower is slave to the lender" (Prov. 22:7, NIV).

The Bible considers debt slavery and a curse. God does not want his children to be ruled over or to be slaves. You are a child of the Most High God, and you have access to all that he owns. But these blessings will be hindered when you're mired in the vicious cycle of debt. Practice obedience and discipline in this area and say "NO!" to debt. Meditate on this truth and commit to eliminating credit cards as a common form of payment for goods and services. Your goal is to be the lender and not the borrower. We will talk more about lending (the opposite of borrowing) in chapter 5.

Exercise 1:

- Stop reading now and go review each of your credit card statements. Write down the finance charges you paid on each card for the past six months. You don't have to calculate it, as it will be clearly shown on your statement as "purchase interest charge" or something similar. Sometimes, seeing the extra money you're throwing away goes a long way to changing the "buy now, pay later" mindset. How can you ever pay these cards off, if a chunk of your payment goes toward the interest charge and not the outstanding balance?

• Commit to stop using credit cards from this day forward for all consumer purchases; either forego the purchase altogether or delay it until you have enough cash to buy it outright.

• Use one of the methods in Appendix B to eliminate your credit card debt. Set a goal to pay off your credit cards and stick to it!

False mindset #2: There will never be enough money.

Often referred to as a poverty mindset, it stems from a place of lack. Perhaps you grew up impoverished or in a household where one or both parents were extremely frugal. You learned early on to hold on tight to money because it's scarce. You've probably been referred to as a "cheapskate," and you wear the banner proudly. You take bargain hunting to the next level and look at everything through the lens of how much it costs. You miss out on things in life because frankly you don't want to spend the money. So, you might ask, "Isn't it good to be conscientious about spending?" "Why would someone with a frugal mindset ever have money problems?" As stated earlier, and as will be discussed in detail in later chapters, you must release money to get money. Someone said it best: "If you are so busy clinching your fist so money can't get out, it can't get in either." There's a delicate balance to be struck.

TRUTH #2: "But my God shall supply all your needs according to his riches in glory by Christ Jesus" (Phil. 4:19).

The truth of the matter is, there is more than enough for everyone! God is the provider and supplier of all your needs, and he is the owner and creator of everything. It is vital that you grasp and embrace this truth, because the mindset trap of "never enough" will become a self-fulfilling prophecy. If you truly think there is never enough, then there will never be enough. But if you have faith that God shall supply all your needs according to *his* riches (not according to yours), then you know that any and every need you have will be met. There is no scarcity. The scarcity mindset is one of the most entrenched, so pray and ask God to help you replace it with his truth.

False mindset #3: I can't rise above my circumstances.

People with this mindset feel resigned to their current financial circumstances. They believe that the way it is, is how it will always be. They do not see a way out. They have no hope or plan to make things better. Unlike mindset 2, they believe there's plenty money out there, but they have no idea how to tap into it. They don't feel like wealth is attainable for them, but rather that they are a victim of their circumstances. Unfortunately, some hold on to this mindset because it removes any responsibility for them to do something different.

TRUTH #3: "I can do all things through Christ who strengthens me" (Phil. 4:13).

This truth totally counters the belief that you can't rise above your circumstances. It promises you that you can do *all* and *anything* with the power of Christ. Not only can you rise above your circumstances, but also you're responsible for doing so. The Scripture says "I" can do all things, not that *he* will do those things for you. He will merely give you the strength to act on your own accord. This Scripture should be adopted for all areas of your life, not just financially; but it certainly works for money too! And since it says you can do "all" things, why not go for the gusto. Think big! Dream big! Enlarge your vision! The loftier the goal, the greater the success even if you don't quite reach it; you'll be better off than you were if you had never tried.

False mindset #4: Creating and following a budget is too hard.

Those who fail to plan, plan to fail. If you bury your head in the sand when it comes to managing your money, your money will manage you. This mindset is usually attributed to a lack of discipline and a disregard for limits. However, it is vital that you regularly (monthly is ideal) assess your income against your expenses, so that you know what's coming in and what's going out. If what's going out is greater than what's coming in, you have a negative bottom line and will have to resort to credit cards and debt to survive day-to-day. There are some great online tools that make budgeting and tracking your money easy. In addition to a short-term (monthly) budget, you should have a long-term plan to consider future needs, including a retirement plan. You're never too young, and it's never too early to start planning for retirement.

TRUTH #4: Suppose one of you wants to build a tower. Won't you first sit down and estimate the cost to see if you have enough money to complete it? For if you lay the foundation and are not able to finish it, everyone who sees it will ridicule you, saying, this person began to build and wasn't able to finish. (Luke 14:28–32, NIV)

These words came from Jesus himself. He is specifically talking about money by saying that we need to make sure we have enough *before* we commit to a thing, anything. But how many of us spend, buy, travel, etc., without comparing what we have coming in with what we have going out. That's all a budget is. It needs to be done on a biweekly or monthly basis. Every time you get paid or receive money, there should already be a plan for what you will do with each dollar, to include saving, investing, eliminating debt, tithing, giving, etc. If it's not in the budget (i.e., the plan), then you don't do it. Not following a budget can lead to ridicule.

False mindset #5: No one would want to pay me for my products or services.

Many of you have talents, skills, and ideas that could be a great source of income! I can't tell you the number of people I see who have a great product, service, or idea that they are giving away for free or for less than its value. Sometimes, you'll be led to help others or to offer your services for free, and you should do just that. But this should be the exception not the rule. If you've been asking God to bless you financially, to enlarge your territory, and to make a way out of no way, then look and see what he has deposited in you to make it happen. The answer might lay in your hands, literally. One thing is clear: wealthy people know the value of what they have to offer, and they demand it. If you don't value what you have to offer, no one will. What's the thing that you can do easier or longer than others, and brings you so much fulfillment that you would do it even if you didn't get paid? That's usually the key to your wealth-generating talent.

TRUTH #5: "And in the same house remain, eating and drinking such things as they give: for the laborer is worthy of his hire. Go not from house to house" (Luke 10:7).

Again, we hear words from Jesus directly in which he is telling laborers that he appointed to go house to house to preach and heal folks, that they are to receive the payment they are given in the form of food and drink. They are worthy of it. And *you* are worthy of payment for your labor, skills, gifts, talents that God has appointed to you. What product, service, or business is inside of you—waiting to be birthed, to be released? There are people out there who need what you have and are willing to pay for it! Know your value!

Exercise 2:

Many beliefs are so buried in our subconscious that we aren't aware of them. Until you become aware of these limiting beliefs, it will be hard to change your mindset. Set aside some quiet time to really focus on this exercise. It can help you uncover your false mindset about money and change it:

- Think about some of your earliest attitudes, thoughts, and beliefs about money. Focus on things you were told, or things you observed your parents say or do when it came to money. Also consider any emotionally charged or dramatic life events associated with money that have left a lasting mark on you. Write down as many as you can.

- As you continue reading the book, come back to your list when you read a biblical principle or Scripture that counters an old thought pattern. Scratch out the old thought or belief and write in the new one.

- Begin to meditate daily on these new principles. In doing so, you will begin to change your mind-set.

Additional Scriptures for study:

- Deuteronomy 8:16–18
- Deuteronomy 10:14
- Psalm 34:9–10
- Psalm 49:16–17
- Proverbs 3:27–28
- Proverbs 28:19
- Romans 13:6–8

CHAPTER 2

$peak Your Way to Wealth

Death and life are in the power
of the tongue: and they that love
it shall eat the fruit thereof.
—Proverbs 18:21

One of my favorite relatives, who I talk to frequently, would often say how "broke" he was. Every conversation with him was peppered with him lamenting, "Man, I'm so broke" and "I don't have enough money," and on and on. He had a decent job but was the sole provider for his family. As such, he never felt he had enough, and I'm sure things were tight, but conversations with him were overwhelming to my ears, and I am sure to others as well. After what seemed like years of this, I finally told him during one of our phone conversations. "Stop saying you are broke! Stop decreeing and declaring that over your life. Even if you really do believe it, there's nothing to be gained from constantly saying it." He was taken aback because I don't think he realized how much he said it, it was so ingrained in him. However, he did stop saying it. Conversations with him from that point on were void of any conversations about money and his lack of it. A short time later, he got offered a position with a six-figure salary. He was able to retire from his current position, which allowed him to earn retirement pay and a salary! He was able to pay for his wife to go back to school full-time to obtain her degree, her lifelong dream, which will ultimately increase her earning potential. His financial position went from "broke" to surplus. I'm not sure if he ever fully made the connection between his words and his circumstance, but I did. I've seen the impact of decreeing and declaring too many times in my and others' lives to not believe in its power.

How many of you are speaking death over your money and literally killing your chances for a financial breakthrough? The Bible says that life and death are in the power of the tongue and that the tongue "corrupts the whole body, sets the whole course of one's life on fire, and is itself on fire by hell" (James 3:6, NIV).

Imagine that, you can literally burn up your money with your tongue!

Your Children Are Listening

I believe that one of the most powerful ways to influence the mindset of your children is by what you say out of your mouth. They may not know the intimate details of your earnings, savings, spending habits, etc., but one thing they will know is what they hear you say about money. If you want to set your children on a good financial path, then watch what you say to and around them regarding money. As a matter of fact, watch what you say about money in general, and you won't have to curb your conversation around them. Plus, you'll be speaking life into your finances. For example, if your children are constantly hearing you complain about the bills, or that there isn't enough money for this and that or that your "paycheck is peanuts," they'll develop a poverty mindset. Now, you want them to have a realistic view of finances and expenses, so you shouldn't sugarcoat your situation, but rather use it to teach them what to do and not to do and let them know that wealth can be theirs. For starters, buy them a copy of this book.

The Bible says, "Train up a child in the way he should go: and when he is old, he will not depart from it" (Prov. 22:6).

"Training up" involves helping them to develop a healthy mindset, including as it pertains to money. It's so much more effective establishing a mindset of truth in them, when you have one.

God Said It, I Believe It, and that Settles it!

Speaking your way to wealth has two components: Repeating what God says about your finances and believing it. One without the other is ineffective. You must confess, according to God's truth, **AND** believe that it will manifest in your life. I've learned that even if the faith isn't quite there yet, if you agree with what God says, by saying it yourself enough times, your faith will catch up. Don't agree with what you see but rather agree with what God says about the situation. Review the scriptures surrounding money throughout the book and at the end of each chapter. Choose ones that address areas in which you are most challenged and begin to meditate on them daily. Anytime you feel yourself getting ready to speak lack, doubt, fear, or dissatisfaction, speak a Scripture instead. It bears repeating: Agree with the Word of God, not with your situation. When you choose to use the power of your tongue to speak God's word, you give life to your situation, and things will begin to shift for the better. Not just the better, but for the good, the great, and the best! If your situation is that you just can't see a way out financially, the more you try, the deeper you seem to get into debt, you seem buried by expenses or if you're tired of having just enough, begin to declare, "I am blessed beyond measure." Decree and declare that you are the son or daughter of the King of kings, and you have access to his riches. Surplus and not lack is your condition.

Exercise 3:

This is a personal challenge. You are to go one full week without speaking any lack or negativity about anyone or anything—not about your finances, your situation, your spouse, your job, your children, the traffic, the long lines at the bank, etc. Speak only positivity. Even if a situation isn't what you want it to be or a person isn't acting as you think they should, speak those things that aren't as though they are. I've had people tell me how hard this assignment is, yet it is very revealing, because once you are conscious of your words, you will discover how often you use your tongue to speak death over a situation, instead of life. I had one client tell me that she started speaking only positive words to her husband, complimenting him and thanking him for things throughout the day. She didn't allow herself to comment on the things he didn't do or do well, or that bothered her. She said after several weeks of this, her husband began to change! Imagine that—you have the power to change others with your words. This works especially well with your children. Whatever you are praying and hoping for them, start speaking it as if it is already the case. And stop speaking the things you don't want for them, even if its what you currently see.

So instead of speaking what you see, speak what it is you want about the situation. Once you master this for one week, try to do it for two weeks, and then a month. Over time, it will become natural for you to choose your words carefully. When this happens, not only will your speech change, but so will your heart, your perspective, your life, and the lives of others.

Additional Scriptures to study:

- Matthew 6:31–32
- James 4:13–15
- Revelation 2:9

CHAPTER 3

$eek Wisdom

*If any of you lack wisdom, you
should ask God, who gives generously
to all without finding fault,
and it will be given to you.*
—James 1:5 (NIV)

A key step to renewing your money mind is to seek wise
and godly counsel. Now this isn't just any counsel, because
as we discussed earlier, society's view of money is opposite of God's and is based on greed, materialism, and get
all you can, however you can. Therefore, following what
society says about money and how to manage it will never
lead to a permanent transformation. The fact that you are
reading this book means you are someone who seeks wisdom. I recommend you take a money class at your church
or read a Bible-based financial book at least twice a year.
Your mind is a muscle and just like other muscles in your
body, if it isn't exercised properly, it gets out of shape and
atrophied. If you do seek a financial adviser, ask if they are

"fiduciary," which means they legally must act in your best interest, as opposed to making a profit for themselves.

As this chapter's opening Scripture states, the best place for us to get wisdom is from God himself. If you ask, he will provide answers freely, as he wants you to know. I've often heard people refer to the Bible as "Basic Instructions Before Leaving Earth." While that's a cute acronym for the word "Bible," God has placed all the answers to the issues of life in his Word because he *does* want us to have answers, information, and wisdom. However, depending on where you are in your walk with Christ, you may not always be able to readily understand what it's saying to you. But if you meditate on God's Word around money, and ask him what he wants you to know, he promises to tell you freely. Most of us don't know, because we don't ask him. How does he tell us? Sometimes, it's through a still, small voice, or through something you read, or a sermon you might hear, or even a friend or family member speaking to you. I know someone who hears God's wisdom through movies. She will see the same movie as others and walk away with all kinds of divine and godly revelation, that they didn't get. It's amazing actually. God has a myriad of ways to answer the questions you have of him, to impart his wisdom to you. Remember, He *wants* you to know. As you receive wisdom, and start applying it, your situation or your perspective of the situation, will change for the better.

Wisdom Leads to Material Blessings

When King Solomon, the wisest man to ever walk the earth, was asked by God what he wanted, he told God, "Give me now wisdom and knowledge, that I may go out and come in before this people: for who can judge this thy people, that is so great?" In other words, Solomon said give me wisdom to help me be the best that I can be at my job, my role as king. And God said to Solomon, since you didn't ask for riches, wealth, honor, death to your enemies, nor long life, but you asked for wisdom and knowledge, I will give you not only wisdom and knowledge, but also riches, wealth, and honor unlike any king before you nor any after you. How about that? God is so pleased with you when you seek wisdom and desire to be the best person you can be to serve others that he will bless you with riches and honor. So not only does he want you to ask for and desire wisdom, but he will give it to you, *and* it comes with lots of other perks and benefits. How can we afford *not* to seek wisdom in our financial affairs and our lives in general?

Wisdom: Practical Applications

Next, let's look at biblical wisdom applied to a few common money questions people ask me most, as a financial counselor. Some of these topics are covered in more detail in other chapters, but let's take a quick look at them now. You'll probably be surprised that the Bible provides wisdom on some of these everyday money issues.

Q. *Should I get a consolidated loan to pay off all my debt?*
A. You can't borrow your way out of debt. While logically it might make sense to get one big loan to pay off several smaller loans, typically it is not wise. All you are doing is switching lenders. You are still a borrower. And what often happens is you end up maxing out

the credit cards again, which leaves you with the consolidated loan *plus* your credit cards with new balances. Most of the credit repair companies and programs prey on people's desperation to get out of debt. However, there's no way to get out of debt quickly. You likely didn't get into debt overnight, and you can't get out of it overnight either. It is a process that requires patience, commitment, diligence, and discipline. But it can be done and should be your number one money priority. Common sense tells you, "It's easier to pay one creditor than many;" however, kingdom sense tells you, "Borrowing is what got you into this mess, so borrowing can never be the solution." Wisdom from the Bible says:

> *"Owe nothing to anyone except to*
> *love and seek the best for one another"*
> (Rom. 13:8, AMP).

Q. *Is it more important to save money or to pay off debt? I can't afford to do both.*

A. You can't afford *not* to do both. If you don't have money saved up and an emergency occurs (like the COVID-19 Pandemic), you'll likely have to use your credit cards or take out a loan to handle it. This is counteractive to your goal of eliminating your debt. Thus, I recommend you work toward accumulating at least three (though six is ideal) months of living expenses, while paying the minimum balances on your credit cards and installment loans. Once you have the three months saved, then you can put more money toward your debt, using one of the debt elimination techniques in

Appendix A. The three months' worth of savings is a great cushion that most people do not have but need desperately. You want to put the money somewhere safe and relatively easy to get to in case you need it in an emergency. Online banks have gotten popular and tend to offer a much higher interest rate than brick and mortar banks. An online bank is a bank without any branch network that offers its services remotely via online, telephone, mail and mobile.[6] Most online banks, like traditional banks, have the backing of the Federal Deposit Insurance Corporation (FDIC). Online banks are covered in more detail in Chapter 5. The key to saving is to be consistent. You should save some amount, no matter how small, from every paycheck using automatic payroll deductions. (We will talk more about automatic deductions in Chapter 5). Something is better than nothing, and the money you are setting aside will add up over time. Otherwise, if you don't save, you can expect your situation in the future to be the same as it is today. The Bible sheds wisdom around saving for a rainy day:

> *"Four things on earth are small, yet they are extremely wise: Ants are creatures of little strength, yet they store up their food in the summer"* (Prov. 30:24–25).

We will talk more about saving in Chapter 5.

Q. *Is it okay to co-sign on a loan for a friend or family member?*
A. No, never! A 2016 CreditCards.com survey of 2,003 US adults revealed that 38 percent of cosigners had to

pay some or all the loan or credit card bill because the primary borrower did not. The survey also reported that 28 percent of the cosigners experienced a drop in their credit score because the person they cosigned for paid late or not at all.[7] The Bible speaks clearly against cosigning.

Typically, the reason someone needs a cosigner is because the lender sees them as a high risk and is not willing to loan them the money without a backup plan. In other words, the lender wants to make sure if the borrower defaults on the loan, the lender has someone else from whom they can collect the money owed them—that would be *you*, if you are a cosigner. So, if you know the person is a high risk, why would you put yourself in that situation? Furthermore, when you cosign, you are contributing to that person's debt problems. You're allowing them to get a loan that they otherwise might not be able to get, thus getting in further financial bondage. Often, parents cosign for a young adult child who hasn't established credit yet. Even in this situation, I recommend you not cosign, but use it as an opportunity to teach your son or daughter about the dangers of debt. Encourage them to save the cash for whatever item they need, even if it's a larger purchase like a car. This will keep them from purchasing beyond their ability. As a loving and supportive parent, you might believe that by cosigning, you're helping your child establish credit, but you're doing so at a risk to yourself. There are other ways for your children to establish credit. For one, they can obtain a secure credit card which uses their own money as their credit limit.

It's interesting that Proverbs, the Wisdom book, speaks against cosigning (surety) in four separate warnings:

1. If you have cosigned for someone, get out of it as quickly as you can:

    > *My son, if you have become surety (guaranteed a debt or obligation) for your neighbor, If you have given your pledge for [the debt of] a stranger or another [outside your family], If you have been snared with the words of your lips, If you have been trapped by the speech of your mouth, do this now, my son, and release yourself [from obligation]; since you have come into the hand of your neighbor, Go humble yourself, and plead with your neighbor [to pay his debt and release you]. Give no [unnecessary]sleep to your eyes, nor slumber to your eyelids; Tear yourself way like a gazelle from the hand of the hunger, and like a bird from the hand of the fowler.* (Prov. 6:1–5, AMP)

2. The way to be financially secure is to hate being someone else's financial security:

    > *"He that is surety for a stranger shall smart for it: and he that hate the suretyship is sure"* (Prov. 11:15).

3. Ignorance causes us to enter into a cosign agreement with a friend:

    "A man void of understanding striketh hands, and becometh surety in the presence of his friend" (Prov. 17:18).

4. If a person's credit is so bad that he can't get a loan, why should he risk impacting yours?

    "If thou has nothing to pay, why should he take away thy bed from under thee?" (Prov. 22:27).

Q. *Should I borrow from my 401K or other retirement account to pay my child's college tuition or debt?*

A. No! There are varying schools of thought on this according to the world, but biblical wisdom says to leave your retirement money alone, which ultimately will provide for your future. Don't borrow against it for any reason!

    "There is precious treasure and oil in the house of the wise (who prepare for the future), but a short-sighted and foolish man swallows it up and wastes it" (Prov. 21:20, AMP).

My very wise father always told me work hard and save while you're young so when you're old, you don't have to work hard, unless that's your desire. When you're young and working age, you have the value of time on your side.

You can't get those years back. Sometimes, you can borrow money from your retirement account, with the stipulation that you must pay it back. However, you're borrowing from yourself, and you can never recoup the interest you lose while your money is pulled from the investment account. It is better to plan for your child's college tuition the moment they are born by purchasing a State 529 Plan, educational IRA or purchasing stocks, bonds or other investment vehicle in their name (more on investing in chapter 5). If your child is nearing college and you don't have the benefit of time to invest and save, then it's better to have your child take out a student loan than for you to borrow the money, because:

- They will have more time to pay it back
- Interest on student loans is significantly lower than parent loans
- They will be investing in their own future. However, let me stress that borrowing should be the *last* resort, and should be done for the least amount needed.

Q. *Is it okay to file bankruptcy?*
A. No, not when it's being used as an "easy" recourse to get out of debt.

> *"The wicked borrows and does not repay, but the righteous give generously"*
> (Ps. 37:21, NIV).

If you file bankruptcy, you are legally declaring that you are unable to pay your debts. However, sometimes a creditor will force you to file bankruptcy to get some portion of the money due them. They're not always able to collect 100 percent of what's owed to them, and they write off the difference as "bad debt expense." As such, some bankruptcy terms can result in you paying back less than the full amount you borrowed. While bankruptcy should be the absolute last resort, keep in mind that it can negatively affect your credit report for up to ten years and possibly could prevent you from getting hired for a job. Bankruptcy is not a good solution for getting out of debt, and it's scripturally unsound.

Q. *Is gambling a sin?*

A. While the Bible doesn't specifically mention gambling, it does say that God is the owner of everything in the earth. You are merely a steward or manager of whatever he's allowed you to possess. Once you give God his 10 percent (more on that in chapter 6), you are expected to manage the remaining 90 percent in a responsible way, according to his principles. Too often, gambling can lead to irresponsibility, an unhealthy pursuit and desire for money, greed, competition, a get-rich-quick mind-set, and even addiction. At the root of all gambling is dependence on luck, fueled by idolatry, which God commands against.

> *"But as for you who forsake the Lord and forget my holy mountain, who spread a table for Fortune and fill bowls of mixed wine for Destiny, I will destine you for the sword, and all of you will fall in the slaughter; for I called you did not answer,*

*I spoke but you did not listen. You did evil
in my sight and chose what displeases me."*
(Isa. 65:11–12, NIV)

As such, any activity that squanders the possessions that God has entrusted to you and that leads you into temptation should be avoided at all costs.

Q. *How much life insurance do I need to have?*
A. Contrary to popular opinion, fueled by Hollywood movies, the purpose of life insurance is *not* to make your loved one a millionaire upon your death. Rather, it is to ensure that he or she can maintain a healthy standard of living when you die. To determine how much life insurance you need, you first need to figure out what obligations (e.g., debts, funeral expense, etc.) and future needs (e.g., children's college) would have been covered by your income. There are several free, online life insurance calculators you can use. After you use one of these tools to estimate the amount of life insurance you need, compare that to your current coverage to determine if you have enough. Many are uncertain whether to buy term life insurance (provides coverage for a specific period of time) or whole life insurance (provides coverage for as long as you live). Financial guru Suze Orman says you should only buy guaranteed level term insurance. She says that permanent insurance policies like whole life insurance are a bad investment.[8] I agree with her wholeheartedly.

Q. *Should I stop paying my tithes to pay off debt?*
A. We haven't really talked about tithes much and will do so in chapter 6, but we still can provide a brief answer to this very popular question now. No!

Q. *I don't have a lot of assets, do I still need a will?*
A. Yes. You want whatever you do have to be distributed according to your desires. However, in addition to a will, you should consider these other powerful ways to guarantee your assets are distributed to your love ones:

1. Joint ownership. Add your heir's name to the deed or title of an asset as part owner
2. Beneficiary designation. For accounts or policies, you can name a beneficiary to receive the asset or benefits upon your death
3. Trust. Allows you to carve out your assets and provide specific instructions regarding who gets what, how, and when. This is particularly common when heirs are minors who may need to be guided and controlled with any inheritance they receive.

These three methods provide for quicker distribution of assets than a will, which will have to go through probate (proved and validated in a court of law) and can be contested. However, even if you use any of the other three methods, it's highly recommended that you still have a will, as it serves as the foundation of your estate planning.

Due to the complexity and importance of estate planning, you should seek the wisdom of an estate planning attorney or professional. Don't delay! The Bible cites the importance of preparing and planning for your death, for the benefit of your loved ones:

> *"In those days was Hezekiah sick
> unto death. And the prophet Isaiah the
> son of Amos came to him and said unto
> him, Thus said the Lord, set thine house
> in order; for thou shalt die, and not live"*
> (2 Kings 20:1).

Q. *Should I collect Social Security as soon as I'm eligible?*

A. There are many schools of thought on this, but most financial experts say it's better to wait until age seventy to collect your Social Security benefits. There's the adage "a bird in the hand is worth two in the bush" so some might ask: "why put off a sure thing, for something that I may not be around to get if I pass away before my seventieth birthday?" Yes, this is true, and whether you file for Social Security at the earliest filing age (sixty-two), depends on several personal factors, such as your health, other income sources, financial needs, et al. However, at this age you receive only 75% of your primary insurance amount. If you wait until your full retirement age (67 for those born in 1960 or after) you'll receive 100% of your primary insurance amount. If you wait until age 70 to file, you'll receive 132% of your primary insurance amount!

Additional Scriptures to study:

- Joshua 1:8
- Proverbs 13:11
- Proverbs 13:22
- Proverbs 20:21
- Proverbs 21:5
- Proverbs 22:26
- John 8:32

CHAPTER 4

$earch Your Heart

For where your treasure is, there
will your heart be also.
—Matthew 6:21

If you want to know what you truly value in life, just look at where you spend your money. As the opening Scripture says, "Where your treasure is, there will your heart be also." We spend money on those things we want, enjoy, and deem important to us. Money is a good indicator of our heart condition. Spiritually, our heart and mind are akin, so how you feel about money is based on your mindset. If you believe that "stuff" can make you happy, then you'll value getting stuff—new stuff, bigger stuff, more and more stuff. There will never be enough. You'll never be satisfied. Lots of people worship "stuff"—all the things that money can buy.

"Come on *Down!*"

I grew up watching the game show, *The Price is Right*, and I always marveled at how people would lose their mind, I mean literally go bonkers, when their name was called to "come on down." They'd run down the aisle hugging strangers and other contestants. When they won the bid, they would bound on stage grabbing the host; and if the announcer revealed they have a chance to win **"A NEW CAR!"** most were moved to hysteria. The game show has been on the air for over forty years and is showing no signs of losing popularity. It's an entertaining show, but it plays directly into the consumerism mindset—offering the chance to win money, cars, trips, appliances, boats, and more. The stuff of which most people dream. The unbridled mania contestants display over the chance to win "stuff" reflects where their hearts are.

There are countless stories about Black Friday (the busiest shopping day of the year)—chaos, fights, and store mobs leading to deaths and injuries. There is even a black-fridaydeathcount.com website where they record that from 2006 to 2018, there have been twelve deaths and 117 injuries across the country. These tragedies are typically the result of people competing to get one of the limited numbers of significantly marked-down consumer products. In 2014, consumers spent nearly $51 billion between Black Friday and Cyber Monday.[9]

At a recent release for the "Rookie of the Year" Air Jordan 1 shoes in China, there was a line of five hundred people at a Nike Store. When one customer tries to cut in front of some people in line, other customers punched and kicked him.[10] The customers were in such a frenzy about the shoe release, no one bothered to stop and help the battered customer. They wanted their "stuff;" that's where their heart was in that moment, not on a suffering human. You probably haven't done anything that drastic, but ask yourself, "Do I ever put the pursuit of material things above people?"

You can't take it with you

Here's a sobering thought regarding "stuff"—everything you own will eventually end up in the junkyard. No matter how bright and shiny it is now, it will rust, rot, and decay. It will end up a rubbled mass because nothing lasts forever. Also, you've never seen a U-Haul truck following a hearse. Once you die, you can't take your money or material things your money has bought with you.

As such, God says:

> "Lay not up for yourselves treasures upon earth, where moth and rust doth corrupt, and where thieves break through and steal: but lay for yourselves treasures in heaven, where neither moth nor rust doth corrupt, and where thieves do not break through nor steal." (Matt. 6:19–20)

To make matters worse, sometimes our "stuff" has made its way to the junkyard or landfill, but we are *still* paying for it on our credit card. That's pure craziness! So, the next time you are about to buy something shiny and new, think about its inevitable ending. Being able to "swipe" to pay has contributed to consumerism because we don't see our money leave our hands. We swipe and in exchange, we get some "stuff." Get to the mindset of paying cash for consumer purchases and services; that way, you can see and feel the full impact of your spending on the things near and dear to your heart. Here's an exercise that will reveal your heart.

Exercise 4:

Using your checkbook (if you use one) or your debit card records, examine your last fifteen transactions. What pattern do you see? For what types of products or services do you see multiple entries? Where's your heart—is it food/eating out, entertainment, technology, God/church, family, friends, etc.? If fifteen entries don't reveal a pattern, look at more, perhaps the entire previous month. I encourage you to do this exercise periodically to search your heart.

Before doing the above exercise, you may not have been conscious of where your heart was, but your money will not lie. For where your treasure is, there will your heart be also. If you want to change the focus of your heart, change where you are placing your money. Here's an example: Let's say that someone you love suffered from Alzheimer's disease. As a result, you decide to start donating to the Alzheimer's Foundation. Before your loved one, you may not have even thought about the disease, let alone donated to its cause. But now, because your heart is there, you're willing to donate money to it. Every time you hear about a development being made in the cure, your ears will perk up because you're vested in it.

The more intentional and conscientious you are about where you place your money, the better balance you will obtain. You won't be mindlessly swiping and accumulating stuff. Since you can't take your stuff with you when you leave this earth, and it's all gonna end up in the junkyard eventually, change your mind about it. Commit to sending it ahead, storing it in heaven, by managing your money in the way God directs you. One way to do that is through giving, which we will talk about extensively in chapter 7.

One of the most common Bible verses regarding your heart toward money that would be good to memorize in its entirety is:

> *"For the love of money is the root of all evil: which while some coveted after, they have erred from the faith, and pierced themselves through with many sorrows. But thou, O man of God, flee these things; and follow after righteousness, godliness, faith, love, patience, meekness."* (1 Tim. 6:9–11)

Another good Scripture to memorize and meditate on if you find that your heart is overly concerned with money is:

> *"No man can serve two masters: for either he will hate the one, and love the other; or else he will hold out the one, and*

*despise the other. Ye cannot serve God and
mammon**"* (Matt. 6:24).

Let's end this chapter with the story about the rich
young man who asked Jesus what he needed to do to be
assured of eternal life. Jesus told him to keep the commandments, to not: murder, commit adultery, steal, bear
false witness, and to honor his father and mother, and to
love his neighbor as himself. The young man, obviously
of good character, wanted to know since he had honored
all those things, what else could he be missing? Then Jesus
truly searched the young man's heart by telling him:

*"If you want to be perfect, go, sell
your possessions and give to the poor, and
you will have treasure in heaven. Then
come, follow me"* (Matt. 19:21, NIV).

The story goes on to say that when the young man
heard this, he went away sad, because he had great wealth.
Even though the young man was living a moral life, keeping the commandments, his heart was far from God. He
loved his possessions more than the idea of following Jesus
and more than eternal life! He was sad because he knew
he was choosing badly, but he couldn't part with his possessions; they owned him. How many of you choose tem-
porary wealth and the pleasures of this world over eternal

---

* A modern-day term for mammon is materialism. Today, society
seems to be serving mammon more and more. Even believers who
love God, don't make Him Lord of their finances. That is a separate area they compartmentalize and hold on to. Release your hold
on money and watch its hold on you be released.

riches? When the encounter with the young man was over, Jesus told his disciples that "it is hard for someone rich to get into the kingdom of heaven." He stressed how hard it is by saying, "It is easier for a camel to go through the eye of a needle than for someone rich to enter the kingdom of God."

Additional Scriptures to study:

- Exodus 20:17
- Deuteronomy 30:15–16
- Deuteronomy 31:20
- Proverbs 23:5
- Ecclesiastes 5:10
- Ecclesiastes 5:13–15
- Matthew 5:23–24
- Mark 8:36
- Luke 6:35
- Luke 12:15–21
- Luke 16:1–14
- Philippians 4:11–13
- 1 Timothy 6:6–8
- Hebrew 13:5

CHAPTER 5

$tart Lending (Invest)

*The rich ruleth over the poor, and the
borrower is servant to the lender.*
—Proverbs 22:7

In chapter 1, we talked extensively about borrowing, debt, and finance charges. In short, when you borrow, you acquire debt and are required to pay interest (a fee) for the convenience of using someone else's money for a period of time. The longer you take to pay back the loan/debt, the more interest you'll pay. Well, lending is the opposite of borrowing. That's no surprise. But what might be a surprise to you is that you can be a lender to large corporations and businesses, not just to your family or friends.

Stock It to Me

When you buy shares of stock in a company, you are basically lending that company your money for them to use in their business with the expectation that you will get a return on your money. You are now also one of the owners of the company. Yes, stocks represent ownership shares. If the company is successful, you'll earn a return on your investment through dividends or capital gains.

Investing in the stock market is not as confusing or difficult as most people think. No longer do you need thousands of dollars for a stockbroker to even look your way. Now, with the creation of so many online stock trading companies, you can be your own broker. Online stock trading or brokerage companies provide an easy-to-use platform where you can buy and sell as much or as little stock as you want. Some even allow you to buy portions of a share at a time until you have enough saved to buy one full share. All have fees associated with online trading (purchasing and selling stock shares), but they are minimal.

While I do not endorse any company, according to an article in stockbrokers.com, here are the five best online brokers for beginners in 2019: TD Ameritrade, Fidelity, E*Trade, Charles Schwab, and Robinhood.[11]

Stocks 101

There are a couple of stock terms you should know:

Dividends – an amount the company pays you based on the number of shares of stock you own, that reflects their earnings or profits. Dividends can be paid to you in cash or you can reinvest them to buy more shares in the company.

Capital gains – the profit you make when you sell the stock you own at a higher price than you bought it. If you sell the stock you own at a lower price than you bought it, you have a capital loss. You must pay tax on any capital gains earned.

Here's a simple example of stock earnings:

You buy five shares of XYZ stock for $100/share for a total cost of 5 × 100 = $500

After holding the shares for a period, the price increases to $120/share

So now your five shares are worth 5 × 120 = $600

Your capital Gains is $100 ($600 – $500)

By investing (being a lender) in the company, you earned $100 on your money (before taxes).

It's important to remember that earning dividends and capital gains are based on how well a company performs and investor demand for their stock. The stock is being purchased and sold on the market every day, which makes the stock market very cyclical—the stock market goes up, down, and back up again, continuously. Since the overall stock market tends to trend upward over time, there's an investment strategy called "buy and hold" in which you buy stocks and hold them for a long period of time, ignoring fluctuations in the market because eventually, the returns will override the declines. Too often, people see the stock market decline and want to go and sell off their stock in a panic, but that's a sure way to realize a capital loss. Rather, you should heed another stock strategy of "buy low and sell high," which means when the stock market is low (stock prices have dropped), you should buy even more shares of that stock.

Pass the Burrito Bowl, Please

A very common question I'm asked about stock investing is, "How do I know in which companies to invest?" It's a very good question, and the answer is simpler than you might think. You don't need a stock expert, you just need to be observant and to ask yourself, "What companies do I really like and what products do I use frequently and can't do without?" Chances are, if you find the value in a product, service or company, others do as well. Most people only think like a consumer, but it helps to adopt an investor mindset. Once you do, you'll see investment opportunities all around you. Here's my real-life example[†]:

In 2008, I noticed every time I went to a Chipotle Mexican Grill restaurant, the lines were nearly out the door, and in some instances, the lines *were* out the door. The chain was just starting to gain popularity so there was only one Chipotle restaurant within a twenty-mile radius of me, and its lines were always long. Customers were not deterred by the long lines, evidenced by them constantly pouring into the restaurant. While I was one of the many faithful customers that frequented the restaurant, I

[†] Please be advised, past performance is neither an indication nor a guarantee of future success.

also recognized and took advantage of this huge investment potential. Customers loved the product, the service was good, the concept of fast casual dining was catching on, and there was plenty of room for growth since there were unlimited number of locations for them to place restaurants.

In 2006, when Chipotle went public (offered stock for sale), the price was $44 per share. So, you could have purchased ten shares for roughly $440. However, at its peak in 2015, Chipotle stock price was $754 per share. So those ten shares you bought for $440 would have been worth $7,540 nine years later. Today, there are about twenty Chipotle restaurants within a twenty-mile radius of me and the share price, after taking a huge hit because of a health scare, has climbed back up to approximately $700 per share. Those that recognized Chipotle's potential for success early on and purchased stock while the price was still affordable benefitted greatly.

Once a company's popularity and success skyrockets, it's usually too expensive to invest in it. As stated earlier, the strategy is to buy stock at a low price and sell at a high price.

This was only an introduction to stock investing, to show you one way to become a lender. If stock investing is an area of interest to you, I recommend you take a class in stock investing or read one of the many detailed books on the subject.

One final thing I want to talk about regarding stock investing is the idea of diversification. The Bible specifically talks about diversifying your assets.

"Invest in seven ventures, yes, in eight; you do not know what disaster may come upon the land" (Eccles. 11:2, NIV).

If you do decide to invest in the stock market, you can reduce your risk of losing money due to economic fluctuations by diversifying your investments. In other words, "Don't put all your eggs in one basket." Invest in a variety of types of assets to reduce the overall riskiness of your investment portfolio. For example, you might invest in stocks, bonds, and cash. Or you can invest in different companies rather than holding stock from a single company. You can also diversify by investing in foreign securities because they tend to be less closely correlated with domestic investments. For example, an economic downturn in the US economy may not affect Europe's economy in the same way. As such, if you experience a downturn in your US investments, you could have an uptake in your European holdings. Another less risky way to invest in the stock market is through mutual funds and exchange traded funds, which have built-in diversity because they represent the stock of a pool of different companies and sectors.

Always remember that with greater opportunities for return on your money come greater risks of loss on your money. Therefore, stock investing isn't for everyone. However, if you're wise, these risks can be minimized, and diversification is one way to do that.

God says we are to be the lenders and not the borrowers. We should be receiving interest on our money, not paying it. *However, please pray and ask God if stock investing is something you should do. Even when you take steps to min-*

imize the risk of investing, the stock market is something of which you have no control. It is based on the ebbs and flows of this world's economy. We always want to be good stewards of God's money which he is allowing us to manage.

Take That to the Bank

A less risky way to save and invest your money is via financial institutions, such as banks and credit unions. You lend the bank the use of your money via savings accounts, money market accounts, certificates of deposit or other vehicles, with the promise that they will pay you interest on the money. Unfortunately, the amount of interest being earned on a regular savings account is minimal. As such, I recommend keeping very little money in a regular savings account and instead look for greater interest-bearing products that banks offer. As mentioned in chapter 3, a new trend growing in popularity is online banks. These are banks that do not have an actual building but rather provide all their services online. Since they don't have the overhead of maintaining their buildings, they can offer low or no fees and higher interest rates on savings accounts than traditional financial institutions. This isn't the same as a traditional bank that offers its customers online service, but rather an online bank can be accessed *only* through the internet. They can be very convenient and are insured by the FDIC the same as traditional banks. While I do not endorse any online bank particularly, (you should do your own research), here are "the best online banks in the US" according to a January 15, 2019 article by Bankrate: Ally Bank, Discover Bank, Salem Five Direct, Radius Bank,

E-Trade Bank, Capitol One 360, iGObanking, CIBC Bank USA, USAA, and BankPurely.[12]

The 8th Wonder of the World

Albert Einstein, who was regarded as a genius, said that the eighth wonder of the world is compound interest. What exactly is compound interest? It's when your interest earns interest. Let's look at a simple example:

Let's say you put $1,000 dollars in an interest-bearing account that offers a 5 percent (.05) annual interest rate. After one year, you'll have earned $50 ($1,000 × .05). You now have $1,050 in your account. That $1,050 is your new principal, and it will earn 5 percent on it, giving you $52.50 (1,050 × .05) at the end of year two. You now have $1,102.50, just from your money sitting in the account. If that same $1,000 had been sitting under your mattress, you would have $1,000 at the end of two years assuming no one found it and spent it for you.

These are relatively small figures just to demonstrate how compound interest works. It's an easy stream of income—to allow your money to make money. The potential for earnings gets greater the larger the amount (principal) you invest, the higher the interest rate offered on your investment, and the longer the period you invest or save your money. So, a key to saving and investing is to find vehicles that are offering good interest rates (again, you must balance this with risk) and to take advantage of time. The sooner you start saving and investing, the better.

In terms of risk, savings accounts are very safe, as most financial institutions, are covered up to $250,000 per depositor by the FDIC. Also, banks typically use the deposits from savings accounts, certificates of deposit, and money market accounts to lend to other customers. They do not use those accounts to invest in the riskier stock market. As such, you get a low (almost no) return on those types of accounts. However, if a bank uses its customers' deposits for more risky vehicles like mutual funds, stocks, bonds, and other securities, it does so only with money from investors who understand the risks.

Never Too Young to Lend

Parents, you should instill the principle of saving and investing in your children at a young age.

When my daughter was ten, I bought her shares of stock in five different companies as a Christmas gift. I made pretty, professional-looking stock certificates for each company, wrapped and tied them with a bow. When she opened the package and saw these five pieces of paper, she looked at me confused and somewhat disappointed. I explained to her that she was now an investor and part owner of these five companies, and that over time, she could make a lot of money. She understood that part very well! She was excited about being owner in these five companies, which I had chosen because of her interests at the time, such as Disney and JetBlue (because of her love of travel). I explained to her how stock investing worked—you buy shares at a certain price, hold on to them, and as the company grows in value, the price of your stock increases. You can then sell them at a higher price than you bought them for a net gain. This changed her mind-set from being merely a consumer to being an investor. Because her treasure was in these companies, she developed a heart (interest) toward them. When she saw an advertisement or the news about one of the companies in which she owned stock, she'd smile proudly and say, "That's my company!" We cashed in a few shares of her stock to help finance her college education; and when she purchased her first home, at age 24, she furnished it with sales of the stock I had bought her as a child. She has incorporated those early lessons into her adult life, investing in real estate, individual stocks, retirement accounts, and mutual funds to name a few.

Don't Be Found Unfaithful

The bottom line is, you must start lending so that your money will grow. God honors this and sees you as a good steward of his resources. Recall the parable of the talents which is summarized below:

> *A man was leaving for a trip and he left money to each of his servants: to one he gave five talents[‡], to another two, and to another one, to each according to his ability. The one who had received five talents traded with them and made five more. The one who had the two talents made two more, but the one who had received the one talent went off and dug a hole in the ground and hid his employ-*

[‡] A talent was an ancient unit of currency; money used by the Romans and Greeks.

er's money. To the ones who doubled their money the master said "Well done, good and faithful servant! You have been faithful with a few things; I will put you in charge of many things. Come and share your master's happiness!" But for the one that hid the one talent he had been given, His Lord called him wicked and slothful and took his one talent and gave it to the servant who now had ten talents. And the unprofitable servant was then cast in outer darkness, where there was weeping and gnashing of teeth. (Matt. 25:14–30)

You own nothing. All that you have has been given to you to manage. God will come back to see what his return is on what he gave you to manage. This includes not just your money, but your time and abilities as well. In the above parable, the Master rewarded the one who went from five to ten talents by giving him the one talent that belonged to the lazy servant. The master didn't give it to the servant who doubled his two talents to four, even though he called him a good servant as well. This implies that to whom much is given, much is required.

It's Never Too Early to Invest

in Your Retirement

We talked a little about 401K plans in chapter 3. The other important tidbit worth mentioning is you should max out your retirement account, whether it's a 401K, thrift savings plan, etc. Whatever the maximum amount you can contribute, do it. If you can't afford to have the maximum withdrawn every payday, at least make sure you are taking full advantage of any matching plan your company offers. Matching is when your company puts a percentage of or the same dollar amount into your retirement account that you do each pay period, usually up to a maximum amount. For example, if your company matches 100 percent up to 5 percent of what you save, then you should be saving 5 percent. If you're only saving 3 percent, you're leaving 2 percent free money on the table! This can make the difference in hundreds of thousands of dollars when you retire. You also want to consider diversifying your investment account by putting some money in a Roth account—withdrawals are tax free, but you don't get the current tax reduction for contributions to the retirement plan. With a traditional retirement account—you get a tax reduction when you make contributions to the retirement plan, but the withdrawals during retirement are taxed.

The Power of Automatic Deductions

The most surefire and easiest way to invest and save your money is through automatic deductions. You should set up a certain amount to go directly from your paycheck to your investment (or savings) account. The great thing about automatic deductions is you never see the money, therefore you never miss it. You get used to managing without it. Meanwhile, it's quietly and steadily accumulating in your account. Start by setting up at least one allotment from your paycheck to an investment or savings account. Once you're comfortable, you might want to increase the

amount going to that account or set up automated allot-
ments to fund other accounts (retirement, emergency savings, vacation, etc). This is a great way to pay yourself first
and to accumulate wealth because it requires no-discipline
or thinking about it. Automatic deduction is a money
management practice that will yield guaranteed benefits.

When my daughter graduated from college she
moved back home, and I talked to her about automatic
deductions. She set up three automatic deductions: one
allotment went to her retirement account, another to a
savings account and the third to an investment account,
which funded a growth mutual fund. Within two years,
she had enough money in the mutual fund for a down
payment on her first home. The savings account covered
emergencies and unplanned expenses, and she continues
to build up her retirement account.

Automatic deduction is a powerful and hassle-free
process that will yield incredible benefits. If you aren't putting money away automatically every payday, you need to
start now!

Additional Scriptures to study:

- Deuteronomy 28:12
- 2 Kings 4:1–7

CHAPTER 6

$urrender God's Portion (Tithe)

If you saw the title of this chapter and were tempted to skip ahead, thank you for fighting against that instinct. Your willingness to read this controversial topic has just lessened the hold money has on your soul. And the more you delve into this chapter, the freer you will become. You'll see that tithing, which many treat with skepticism, cynicism, or hostility, isn't a burden, but rather a joy that should be viewed with expectation, promise, and freedom! Can you feel the shackles falling off you already?

Why does tithing have such a bad rap? Why do people go to such great lengths to deny, redefine, and ignore God's principle? I believe it's because tithing infringes upon the thing that people love with all their heart, soul, and mind—money. The Bible says that "the love of money is the root of all evil." Imagine, any and every evil you can perceive of begins with mankind's love of money. Wow, that's heavy! Ironically, tithing is one of the most effective things you can do to lessen money's hold on you, to pull evil from the root of your heart, and to help create contentment in your heart. Giving, including tithing, is what I was referring to in the book's introduction when I said: "Getting money isn't the key to wealth, keeping it is; but to keep money, you must let go of it." Tithing (returning to God his portion) is the most important way to let go of money. "It's not that you HAVE to tithe, but rather that you GET to tithe." You get an opportunity to give God back a mere portion of ALL that he has used to bless you. Let's examine more closely.

Important: Before you read any further, stop and ask God to help you grasp the truth and to give you fresh revelation into this topic.

Invest in God

In the previous chapter, we talked about investing and getting a return on your money. Well, tithing is nothing more than making an investment in God. He promises that if you return to him a tithe (10 percent) of all your earnings, he will multiply your money; so much so that you won't be able to store it all. This guarantee isn't backed by FDIC, but by the infallible, inerrant Word of the one who owns it all!

But why does God want us to invest 10 percent of our earnings into him? Surely, he doesn't need our money since *everything* belongs to him anyway! No, it is because he wants to develop discipline in us. He wants us to use our free will to show that we love, trust and obey him. Whenever you see a doctrine, word, or concept mentioned for the first time in the Bible, it shows God's clearest, simplest, and most original intent. This is called the "Law of First Mention." Let's look at the very first time God set aside a portion of his resources from mankind.

The Forbidden Fruit

God always sets aside a portion of what he gives us for himself. It's not that he needs anything from us, but he wants to develop discipline in us; he wants us to exercise our free will on his behalf. In the Garden of Eden, God told Adam and Eve they could eat from every tree of the garden, except one. I'm sure if you're like me, you've scratched your head and wondered, "How come Adam and Eve couldn't avoid that one tree when they had the entire garden at their disposal?"

Truth be told, you might even be a little indignant with them when you think about how their one act of disobedience, defiance, and mismanagement of God's resources led to such tragic circumstances for all of mankind. Now hear this: You demonstrate that exact disobedience, defiance, and mismanagement of God's resources every time you forgo the tithe! He allows you to keep 90 percent of all that you earn, but just like Adam and Eve, it's not enough. You want the 10 percent too, the forbidden fruit. Just like Satan did with Eve, we justify why its ok to keep God's portion. And you know how things turned out for Adam, Eve, and the serpent (Satan).

Reasons People Do Not Tithe

Given God's promises with tithing, why do so few people do it? I've heard many reasons over the years. Here are five of the most common ones and counterpoints for your consideration:

Reason 1: "I Can't Afford to Tithe."

One of the best explanations I've ever heard on the importance of tithing came from Pastor Ron Carpenter's (Redemption Church) sermon series entitled "Supervision" (Parts 1–3). He breaks down the principle in such a simple and practical manner, you can't deny its truths. One of the points he makes is:

Giving God 10 percent (a tithe) that is already his sanctifies the other 90 percent (your seed) and protects it from the devourer. It sanctifies your money that is mingled in the world's system which is marked by lack, greed, and never enough.

So to those that say they can't afford to tithe, I'd like to suggest that you can't afford *not* to tithe. Failure to tithe leaves your remaining money (the 90 percent) open to the devil's fiery darts, and you'll always suffer from a sense of lack, wanting more, and greed. When you tithe, you show God that you trust Him and are a good manager of his resources, and he rewards good management by giving even more.

Luke 16:10 states "Whoever can be trusted with very little can also be trusted with much, and whoever is dishonest with very little will also be dishonest with much." If God can't trust you with the 10 percent, how can he trust you with the 90 percent? Think about it; would you trust your possessions with someone that has proven to be untrustworthy?

Reason 2: "Tithing Is Not in the New Testament."

Comparing the Old Testament (law) to the New Testament (grace) is one of the most popular excuses people give for not tithing. However, the entire Bible is the inspired Word of God. We see examples of the tithe with Adam, Cain, Abel, Abraham, and Jacob, to name a few—all of which came before the law of Moses. Even if the tithe is considered a law of sorts. Jesus himself said that he did not come to destroy the law but to fulfill it. God, not man, established the tithe. The Lord said, "Bring ye all the tithe into my storehouse…" The important point to remember is the tithe is so much more than a law, doctrine, or principle. It is God's *promise*! He said to try him by tithing and see if he won't bless you abundantly. His promises still stand.

Reason 3: "Giving Should Be from the Heart, Not Coerced."

Yes, giving should be from the heart, and yes, "the Lord loves a cheerful giver"; but giving in this context starts after the tithe. The tithe belongs to God, and we are mandated to return it to him. If we don't, God says we are robbing him. God knew that money would have a stronghold on mankind. As a matter of fact, the Bible states that "No one can serve two masters. Either you will hate the one and love the other, or you will be devoted to the one and despise the other. You cannot serve both God and money." Matt 6:24 (NIV) How can you ensure that money doesn't become your master? By tithing. It is a way of escape. Tithing softens our heart and loosens money's hold on our soul.

Reason 4: "I Don't Trust What the Pastor/Church Does with My Money."

The local church needs your support, and I believe that you should tithe where you are being spiritually fed and where God's purpose is at work. Why wouldn't you want to bless the place or person that's been a blessing to you? After all, you can't receive week after week and not give back. However, this is very important: Tithing is *not* between you and the church or you and the Pastor; it's between you and God. Therefore, you must tithe in obedience to God without worrying about what happens to your money; leave that up to God. Yep, even if your pastor drives a Rolls Royce and you drive a fifteen-year-old jalopy, if that's the place where you're being spiritually fed, tithe.

Trust me, God will deal with leaders who lack integrity. Please note that just because a pastor or leader is prosperous, it does not mean they lack integrity. More than likely he or she is a good manager of his or her personal finances and has tapped into the principles of kingdom wealth. If this is the case, you should want to be under their leadership, because oil falls from the head to the body. I don't know about you, but I want to see the evidence of what's being preached in the life of the preacher. So don't be too quick to judge or begrudge the financial prosperity of church leaders.

On the flip side, church leaders must teach what the Bible says about tithing and money and not be afraid to touch the subject. However, we must do it with love, patience, and the leading of the Holy Spirit. We can't guilt people into giving or make them feel condemned when they don't. Allow people to grow in faith and understanding of God's truth. This approach, combined with good old-fashioned prayer, will go a long way in ensuring your church is free from the spirit of lack, greed, and never enough.

Reason 5: "I Don't Believe in Tithing."

Whether you believe in it or not, the promise works for anyone that works it. Let's look at Bill Gates who has an estimated wealth of $65 billion. While he may not use the word "tithing" he has said in a 2013 interview "I have no use for money. This is God's work."[§] As of that interview, he and his wife had given away $28 billion via their charitable foundation (nearly 43% of his estimated wealth). The Gates have activated the promise of abundance in their lives.

Let's look at an analogy: The law of gravity says if you drop a pencil, it's going to fall to the ground. It doesn't matter who drops the pencil, the law of gravity must be fulfilled. So it is with the principle of tithing. Whoever follows it will reap the promise. Now don't get me wrong, when you tithe, financial problems may still occur, but those problems will not devour you. You will be able to handle them. God will make provision. I and countless others I know are witnesses to this. When I didn't tithe or

---

[§] *The Telegraph* Bill Gates interview: I have no use for money. This is God's work. By Neil Tweedie, 9:38pm GMT 18 Jan 2013 www.telegraph.co.uk

whenever I would stop for periods of time, my financial problems became insurmountable. It would be one thing after another. I couldn't ever quite get solid footing and could never seem to get and stay ahead.

Final Thought on Tithing

Tithing is the first and most important step to faithfully managing God's resources, and it comes with a promise that he'll protect your seed (the other 90 percent of your income) from being eaten up. However, tithing is not a get out of jail free card which allows you to disregard everything else. Jesus specifically spoke against this kind of behavior, calling it hypocritical. He said you should tithe, but don't neglect more important things such as justice, mercy, and faith. So while tithing is a key wealth principle, I challenge those who want more to do more. If you want to see abundance flow in your life, if you want to achieve kingdom wealth, both tangible and intangible, then manage all your money well. Be found faithful in all that God has entrusted to you. This includes giving or sowing into others, which we will talk about next. And remember, tithing is more than a law, doctrine, or principal; it is God's promise, which will never fail!

Additional Scriptures to study:

- Genesis 14:20
- Genesis 28:22
- Proverbs 3:9–10
- Malachi 3:11–12
- Luke 20:22–25
- 1 Corinthians 4:2
- 1 Corinthians 16:2

CHAPTER 7

$ow into Others (Give)

What does it mean to sow?

Dictionary.com defines *sow* as a verb meaning "plant (seed) by scattering it on or in the earth." That's exactly what we do with our money. We plant it into worthwhile causes on the earth to be fruitful, which is the part of God's command to Adam and Eve. "Be fruitful and multiply" (Gen. 1:28).

We sow by giving to others. You must decide in your heart how much to give; and don't give reluctantly, or in response to pressure. There are more Scriptures on giving in the Bible than any other money topic. God uses us as his hands and heart on earth to give to those in need. When those who have, give to those who don't have, it keeps the loving balance that God intended. He blesses us in order that we may bless others. It is not for us to store up, hoard, or spend for ourselves. One way to shake off selfishness and money frustrations is to give to others; for in giving, you always receive.

"For God loves a person who gives cheerfully. And God will generously provide all you need. Then you will always have everything you need, and plenty left over to share with others" (2 Cor. 9:7–8, NIV)

Sow into Fertile Ground

Most people understand the need to give to those who are less fortunate than them, but there's a need to give to people who may be doing better than you or who may not appear to have any financial needs. It's also wise to sow into people who have already achieved the same thing that you are trying to achieve. It could be role models, mentors, leaders, etc. One sure way of sowing is by giving tangibly to those who bless you spiritually. Tithing is giving God back his portion, 10 percent. But sowing is taking from your seed (the 90 percent) and planting it into fertile ground. Fertile ground could be a ministry, preacher, pastor, or spiritual teacher that pours into you. You should honor them with love offerings. You should always sow where you flow spiritually. Again, this is separate from tithing. If someone constantly pours into you, elevating your life, and you continue to take what they offer, never giving back to them, the relationship is one-sided. No one-sided relationship can last forever; it will not be at its maximum effectiveness. For example, if you're going to a church week after week and your pastor or spiritual leaders are teaching you, training you, nurturing you, making a positive difference in your life, you should be a tangible blessing to them. You're not paying them for their service, but rather acknowledging your appreciation and respect for their anointing. That is why the Bible *specifically* tells us to bless those that teach us:

> *"Those who are taught the word of God should provide for their teachers, sharing all good things with them"* (Gal. 6:6, NIV).

You should also sow into them with words of affirmation by telling them how their messages and leadership have positively impacted your life. They are anointed and doing the work of God, but they are still human, and they need to be edified and encouraged. As a matter of fact, they may need it even more than those to whom they minister, because the enemy often tries to make them doubt their effectiveness. Leaders need to know that what they are doing is having an impact and making a difference in your life. God's Word tells us:

> *"Therefore encourage one another and build each other up, just as in fact you are doing"* (1 Thess. 5:11, NIV).

If you are being spiritually fed and taught by someone but not sowing into them, begin doing so. The amount isn't so important, but rather the thought and intent behind the love offering. Make up in your mind that you are going to bless the spiritual leaders that God has put in your life. When you bless your spiritual head, you get blessed because the anointing and blessings flow from the head to the body.

$OW INTO OTHERS (GIVE)

Sow into Those in Need

You should always give to those less fortunate than you. God uses you to bless others. He gives you resources and money not to hoard and use solely on yourself, but to meet the needs of those without. You should treat your money like a river, allowing it to flow through you to others. Unfortunately, too many treat their money like a pond, never circulating it; in which case, it becomes stagnant, stale, and contaminated. No matter how bad you think you are doing financially, there is always someone in worse shape than you. There are countless ways and opportunities to sow into others.

> *"Jesus himself said 'it is more blessed to give than to receive'"* (Acts 20:35, NIV).

When we give to those in need or those less fortunate than us, we increase our intimacy with God and our knowledge of him. When we give to others, we are giving to God. Let's see what Jesus said about giving to those in need:

> *Then the righteous will answer him, Lord, when did we see you hungry and feed you, or thirsty and give you something to drink? When did we see you a stranger and invite you in, or needing clothes and clothe you? When did we see you sick or in prison and go to visit you? The King will reply, Truly I tell you, whatever you did*

87

for one of the least of these brothers and sisters of mine, you did for me. (Matt. 25:31–40, NIV)

Sowing Softens the Heart

Too often, people with an unrenewed money mind think that to get ahead financially or otherwise, someone else must lose. Another way of saying this is when you see others going after the same thing you're going after, you feel a competitive or jealous spirit come over you. You feel like if they get ahead, it will lessen your opportunity or take away from you. As such, we consciously or subconsciously try and block their blessings. This is the crabs in the barrel mentality. When one crab is rising to the top of the barrel to escape, another crab still near the bottom pulls him down. I've heard this cliché before, but as I write about it now, I wonder if the crab in the pot was trying to pull himself up and not pull the other crab down. However, the crab in the barrel was unsuccessful because the crab climbing to the top wasn't secure and stable himself. Perhaps, in this analogy, the ideal situation would be for the crab at the bottom to help the other crab get all the way to the top, and then when he's completely secure, he can reach back down and pull up the crab still in the barrel. One of the best ways to combat the green-eyed monster is to support the person of whom you're jealous or in competition. This is not the way the world does things; but as I said earlier, God's kingdom operates totally opposite of the world. While you can also give of your time and talent to support someone, we are specifically referring to a financial blessing in this instance. In so doing, you will be blessed. The Bible tells us that whatever you make happen for others, God will make happen for you.

> *"Knowing that whatsoever good thing any man doeth, the same shall he receive of the Lord, whether he be bond or free"* (Eph. 6:8).

Sow from the Heart

With tithing, we are told to give at least 10 percent, but with offerings, we aren't given an amount, so you should let the Lord lead you. And whatever amount you're led to give, do it with a smile and genuine heart, even if you think it's more than you can afford to give. The Bible says:

> *"Every man according as he purposeth in his heart, so let him give; not grudgingly or of necessity: for God loveth a cheerful giver"* (2 Cor. 9:7).

As a matter of fact, Jesus cares most about the heart with which you give. This is demonstrated in the story of the widow. Jesus watched a crowd putting their money into the temple treasurer. Many rich people threw in large amounts. But a poor widow came and put in two very small copper coins, worth only a few cents. Jesus told his disciples:

> *"Truly I tell you, this poor widow has put more into the treasury than all the*

others. They gave out of their wealth; but she out of her poverty, put in everything— all she had to live on" (Mark 12:41–44, NIV).

Giving in love is crucial, for the Bible says:

"If I give all my possessions to feed the poor…but do not have love, it profits me nothing" (1 Cor. 13:3, NIV).

Any farmer will tell you that to reap a harvest, you must first sow seeds. The richer and more fertile the ground, the better. So, let God direct you where and when to sow. Hear from him. God says:

"Remember this: Whoever sows sparingly will also reap sparingly, and whoever sows generously will also reap generously" (2 Cor. 9:6, NIV).

Where are you sowing? Where are you planting seeds and what is growing from it? If you are not sowing on fertile or good ground, you will not see a harvest, or it will be a harvest of rotten fruit—things that you do not want in your life: stress, worry, discord, lack, negativity, and ungodly things. You will reap what you sow. And as we said in Chapter 4, where you sow is where your heart will be.

Exercise 5:

Commit to looking for ways you can sow into others every day for seven days straight. Ask the Lord to show you needs around you, whether friends, family, or strangers. When he shows you, be obedient and cheerful. Stay open to whatever God may do, don't limit him to your human understanding. Keep a journal of your giving. What is God revealing to you through giving? Repeat this often, and soon, sowing into others will become as natural for you as breathing. God will bless you!

Renewed Money Minds

After reading this study, it is my prayer and desire that you learned something and are inspired to change the way you think about and handle money. I encourage you to pick at least one thing you can do to improve your financial situation and start today! After you've mastered that one thing, revisit the book and pick another. This will allow the concepts to take root. Sometimes, if you try to do too much too soon, you get frustrated and end up not doing any of it. So be patient; but be diligent and committed. Before you know it, your money mind will be renewed, and your common cents will become kingdom wealth!

Additional Scriptures to study:

- Deuteronomy 15:7–8, 10–11
- Deuteronomy 24:14–15
- Psalm 37:21
- Proverbs 11:24–26
- Proverbs 21:13
- Proverbs 28:27
- Isaiah 58:7, 10
- Ezekiel 16:49–50
- Matthew 6:1–4
- Matthew 10:41
- Matthew 13:22
- Matthew 19:23–24
- Luke 12:33-34
- Luke 14:33
- Luke 16:19–31
- Acts 20:35
- 2 Corinthians 8:1–5
- 2 Corinthians 9:7–8
- Galatians 2:9–10
- 1 Timothy 6:17–19

APPENDIX A

Car Buying Hints

1. Shop around for the lowest interest rates, which are usually offered by credit unions or your personal bank. Very seldom will the dealership's financing offer you a better deal, even when they say "special incentives."

2. Get preapproved so that you know your spending ceiling when you walk into the dealership. It also gives you a bargaining chip. If the dealership wants to finance your car, they'll have to give you a better rate than your preapproval. Additionally, when you bring a preapproval letter, the dealership knows that you are a serious purchaser who can take your business somewhere else if your requirements are not met. Places like CarMax market themselves as "haggle-free"—not playing pricing games and offering one fair price. You still need to do your homework and shop around.

3. Don't buy the car from the first dealership you go to, rather use that salesman to learn everything

you can about the car. Ask about the car's features, performance, maintenance, warranty, manufacturer's suggested retail price, the markup, etc. Now, take this knowledge to another dealership and the salesman will see how knowledgeable you are about the car, which will level the playing field.

4. Your warranty should cover the period of finance. If you're financing your car for three years, you need at least a three-year warranty (even if it means buying an extended warranty). You don't want a car note *and* car repair costs. Once the car is paid for (and the warranty is over), you should take part of the monthly note you were paying and put it toward a car maintenance and repair account. Car repairs are a common cause of maxed out credit cards, because they're usually emergency or unplanned situations.

5. You should keep your car once it's paid in full for at least as many years that you financed it, but the more, the better. For example, if you financed your car for three years, then you should keep it another three years after it is paid off to recoup the value. That's six years altogether. However, I typically keep my cars for double digit years, if the value is greater than their expense (the maintenance and upkeep). Too many people buy a new car as soon as they pay off their current one, or even before they pay off their current one. They are essentially financing cars in perpetuity.

6. For this same reason, you should almost never lease a car! If you do, you'll throw away thou-

sands of dollars over the course of several years and have nothing to show for it in the end. Most dealerships offer very creative leasing deals; but at the end of the lease term, you walk away with nothing. There are some exceptions, such as people who have a business or are eligible to write-off certain vehicle costs.

Debt Elimination Plan: The Snowball Method

There are several methods for eliminating debt, but I like this one best because you more quickly obtain a sense of accomplishment (paying off the smallest debt first), which will motivate you to continue the plan.

1. Determine if you truly want to be debt free.

    If you haven't made up in your mind that you're tired of living this way, then you're not ready. It's easy to make a plan, but hard to stick to it if you're not fully committed. It will take discipline. That brings us to the second step.

2. Pray.

    Seek God's help and guidance to give you strength to stick with the plan, for wisdom to make good choices, and discipline to control your spending. It may seem hard and even impossible initially, but decree and declare the following:

"I can do all things through Christ, which strengtheneth me" (Phil. 4:13).

3. Make a list of *all* your debts.

    This list should include all your credit cards, car loans, student loans, home equity loans, medical debts, money owed to family or friends. For each one, describe:
    a. Amount owed
    b. Due date
    c. Interest rate being paid
4. Order the list from smallest debt owed to greatest. This will be the order you pay off your debt.

    (Another method is to order the list from the highest interest rate to the lowest interest rate and pay off the highest first, then move to the next highest, and so on. The debt payment method you choose is totally up to you).

    Make the minimum payment on all your debt but focus on increasing (doubling or even tripling) the payment of your smallest debt first.

    After you pay off the smallest debt, apply what you were paying on it toward the next smallest one. After the second debt is paid off, apply what you were paying on the first and second toward the third smallest debt, and so on.

5. Set a household budget (see false mind-set 4 from chapter 1)

    To eliminate debt once and for all, you must set and stick to a household budget. This will reveal areas where you can cut extra spending, which can help you eliminate debt even quicker. There are lots of great budget apps and tools you can use to do this electronically; or the paper and pencil technique is just as effective. In addition to finding and using a good budgeting tool, consider the following:

    a. Can you do away with some of your luxuries, like getting nails and hair done, going out to dinner or movies?

    b. Can you lower some of your expenses? Sometimes, you can call your cable or phone company and negotiate lower rates as a reward for being a loyal customer.

    c. Use coupons when you shop for groceries or household items

    d. Consider downsizing from larger homes, expensive cars, other major lifestyle changes.

    e. What expensive assets can you sell that would be financially profitable?

    f. Consider a part-time job or side business selling a product or service that your talent provides

        Whatever money you free up each month or at any given time, put toward your debt.

6. Stop using credit and start paying with cash only (see false mind-set 1 in chapter 1). Remove all credit cards from your wallet purse. Hide them,

tear them up, or whatever you must do to stop relying on them.

7. Establish a savings plan.

You need to let your money work for you by saving and investing; and plan for major emergencies so that you do not have to resort back to borrowing as discussed in chapter 5.

8. Establish a giving plan.

This should include tithing and sowing as discussed in chapters 6 and 7.

9. Finally, and most importantly, learn to be content with what you have.

Discontentment is a great cause of spending beyond our means, which leads to debt and financial bondage. Meditate on the Scriptures related to contentment and debt to help you renew your money mind about this topic.

NOTES

1   Rose Publishing. "Trivia: How Many Verses in the Bible Are About Money?" [Blog post]. Feb 8, 2016. Retrieved from Rose-Publishing.com

2   Hess, Abigail. "Here's Why Lottery Winners Go Broke." Last modified 3:28 PM ET Fri, August 25, 2017. CNBC.com

3   Brooks, Rodney. "Why Do So Many Pros Go Broke?" Last modified March 24, 2017. The Undefeated.com.

4   Konkel, Lindsey. "Life for the Average Family." Last modified April 19, 2018. https://www.history.com.

5   Conti, Regina. (primary contributor). "Delay of Gratification – Psychology." Last modified November 4, 2014. https://www.britannica.com.

6   "Direct Bank," *Wikipedia*. https://en.wikipedia.org/wiki/Direct bank.

7   Kossman, Sienna. "Poll:4 in 10 Co-Signers Lose Money." Published: June 5, 2016. Creditcards.com.

8   Cecil, Adam. "What Does Suze Orman Think About Term and Whole Life Insurance?" Last modified January 18, 2018. https://www.policygenius.com.

9   Vivenetto, Gina. "The Madness of the Crowds: The Psychology Behind Black Friday." Last modified November 27, 2015. https://www.today.com.

10   Destefano, Mike. "Watch What Happens When Someone Tries to Cut the Line for Air Jordans" Release in China Gets Heated. Last modified December 13, 2018. Solecollector.com.

11   Reinskensmeyer, Blain. "Best Brokerages for Beginners 2019." Last modified February 18, 2019. https://www.stockbrokers.com.

12   Dixon, Amanda. "Bankrate's Best Banks: The Best Online Banks in the US." Last modified January 15, 2019. https://www.bankrate.com.

CPSIA information can be obtained
at www.ICGtesting.com
Printed in the USA
BVHW080739200122
626620BV00006B/512